Midlife Business Ideas: Kindle Publishing

How to Create a Passive Income with a Kindle Publishing Business

© Copyright 2018 by Quinton David - All rights reserved.

The following eBook is reproduced below with the goal of providing information that is as accurate and reliable as possible. Regardless, purchasing this eBook can be seen as consent to the fact that both the publisher and the author of this book are in no way experts on the topics discussed within and that any recommendations or suggestions that are made herein are for entertainment purposes only. Professionals should be consulted as needed prior to undertaking any of the action endorsed herein.

This declaration is deemed fair and valid by both the American Bar Association and the Committee of Publishers Association and is legally binding throughout the United States.

Furthermore, the transmission, duplication, or reproduction of any of the following work including specific information will be considered an illegal act irrespective of if it is done electronically or in print. This extends to creating a secondary or tertiary copy of the work or a recorded copy and is only allowed with the express written consent from the Publisher. All additional right reserved.

The information in the following pages is broadly considered a truthful and accurate account of facts and as such, any inattention, use, or misuse of the information in question by the reader will render any resulting actions solely under their purview. There are no scenarios in which the publisher or the original author of this work can be in any fashion deemed liable for any hardship or damages that may befall them after undertaking information described herein.

Additionally, the information in the following pages is intended only for informational purposes and should thus be thought of as universal. As befitting its nature, it is presented without assurance regarding its prolonged validity or interim quality. Trademarks that are mentioned are done without written consent and can in no way be considered an endorsement from the trademark holder.

The Midlife Business Ideas Series

The Midlife Business Idea Series is aimed at people between the ages of 30 – 50 that have always wanted to start a business and create freedom in their life. Building a business when you have responsibilities is very different from starting a business when you are care free in your early 20's. You can't afford to put everything you worked for at risk like your family, career and lifestyle.
That is exactly why the Midlife Business Idea series of books will focus on businesses that have 3 characteristics.

1. Easy To Start
2. Can be run part time
3. Create a passive income

The books are geared to be the start of your research process they are quick and easy to read or listen to (Get Audio version for free when you try a FREE Trial on Audible)
The information will help you clarify and decide if a business model is something you should pursue and how to get started.

Table of Contents

Introduction
Chapter 1: Self-Publishing 101
Chapter 2: How to Get a High-quality Cover for Your Book
    Three Ways to Make a Beautiful Cover
Chapter 3: How to Write a Powerful Description
    Practical Tips for Writing a Book Description on Amazon
Chapter 4: Keep the Publishing Business Going
    Professional Training
    Create Partnerships
Chapter 5: How to market your book using social media
    How to Use Facebook at Its Best
        How to Create a Facebook Marketing Strategy That Works?
        Facebook for Small Publishing Businesses
        The Definition of the Goals
Chapter 6: Why Kindle Publishing is the Best Business to Start Today
Conclusion

Introduction

Congratulations on purchasing *Midlife Business Ideas: Kindle Publishing, How to Create a Passive Income with a Kindle Publishing Business* and thank you for doing so. The world of self-publishing is growing increasingly chaotic. Downloading this book is the first step that you can take towards doing something about your financial situation. The first step will not always be the easiest, which is why the information you will find in the following chapters is so important to take to heart, as they are not concepts that can be put into action immediately. If you file these concepts away for when you need them, when the time comes to actually use them, you will be glad you have them at hand.

The following chapters will discuss the primary preparedness principles that you will need to consider if you ever hope to really make money with self-publishing. This means that you will want to consider the quality of your books, including the potential issues raised by their number of words, how to bundle them together, as well as various tools you might need to keep your mind focused on the task at hand.

With those out of the way, you will then learn everything that you need to know about royalties and cover creation. Rounding out the three primary requirements for successful self-publishing, you will then learn about crucial techniques that will further help you in your journey.

I am happy to welcome you to the world of Kindle publishing and to help you to make more money.

Chapter 1: Why Kindle Publishing is the Best Business to Start Today

Numerous factors make self-publishing one of the best businesses to start when you want to break free from the 9 to 5. Here are a few of them.

2. You can do it at home. This is a significant aspect since most people that are moving their first steps in the entrepreneurial world do not have time to go out there and start something. Kindle Publishing allows you to work from home or from anywhere, which makes it perfect for building this business on the go.

3. Passive income. Kindle publishing is the best way to start getting passive income. This means that once you have published your book, money will begin to flow into your pocket without you doing anything anymore. This is very important not only on an emotional level as it helps you to believe and see that you can make money while you are sleeping but on a practical one too: cash flow is fundamental, and self-publishing provides you with that.

4. Low startup costs. Most businesses require a lot of capital to start. However, with Kindle Publishing, you can begin your journey with a few hundred dollars. This makes it easy to start, and in case you lose some money at the beginning, you are not damaging your life savings.

5. Take advantage of Amazon. With Kindle publishing, you are not building anything from scratch, but you are taking advantage of one of the biggest platforms in the world: Amazon. With millions of sales made every day, you are a few clicks away from being successful.

6. Beyond publishing. Starting with Kindle publishing allows you to build the foundations to expand beyond Amazon and beyond books. Why? Because it will enable you to build an audience of readers that are looking for more content, for an environment where they can share their passion. This is why a lot of publishers get into e-commerce, affiliate marketing, or courses: they are the next step to financial freedom.

Chapter 2: Self-Publishing 101

If you are an aspiring writer and would like to sell your first works online or just someone that likes the royalty business model, then Amazon is your best resource. If you want to distribute your books in electronic format, it is one of the best solutions you can find. It has a large audience and allows you to do everything in no time. Just think about it. You are reading a book that you probably bought on the most popular e-commerce in the world and I, as an author, leveraged this possibility to make money.

One thing that a lot of people think is the fact that there is a lot of work required in writing and publishing a book. Well, the truth is that it is not as complicated as it may seem. In fact, what most publishers personally recommend (and do) is to outsource the writing of the manuscript to a writing company or a freelance. You will be surprised to learn that you can get a high-quality book written for around 250 dollars.

Now, it is time to see how to properly publish your book on Amazon.

By following this guide we are about to propose, you can find out how you can publish a book on Amazon in a totally free way and have your book for sale at the price you want within twenty-four hours. Try it and good luck in your career as a writer!

Before seeing in detail how you can publish a book on Amazon, you have to do a couple of fundamental operations. First of all, if you have not done it yet, you have to register on Amazon for free. It takes only a few seconds, and I assume that you are already familiar with the platform.

Next, you must prepare your book for publication on Amazon by trying to comply with all the parameters required for its layout (index, chapters, cover, etc.). You can find all the information you need in the official Amazon guide to prepare books in electronic format. The most common types of digital documents are supported, but it is recommended to use the HTML format or Word DOC/DOCX.

After signing up to the site and preparing your masterpiece for good, you can publish a book on Amazon by visiting Amazon Direct Publishing. Then, log in with your Amazon account information and complete your profile information by clicking on the Update link at the top. You will need to fill in two forms — one with your personal information (name, address, and telephone number) and one with your tax information (you must clarify if you are a private individual or a company, indicate if you are a US citizen, and answer other questions that will allow you to validate your identity and proceed with the publication of the book).

After having provided Amazon with all the requested data, go back to the initial page of the Direct Publishing Service and click on the "Add a new title" button to start publishing your e-book. Then, fill out the form that is proposed to you with all the information related to your work such as title, description, cover, genre, selling price to the public, etc., and click on the "Save and Continue" button to complete the book publishing process.

As for the economic side of the issue, the publication of books on Amazon is free and you can collect royalties for a total of 70% on the sales of the book if you choose a price between 2.99 and 9.99 dollars or 35% if prices between 0.99 and 199.99 dollars are chosen (in every market). You can also join the KDP Select program that allows you to expand the availability of the book to the international versions of Amazon and get some money even from the loan of the work (while maintaining exclusivity on the digital publishing of the book).

Once you have gone through the process, you will then just have to wait up to a day, and then, your book will be live. Most guides end here, but I want to give you some more insights on what to do to extrapolate the most amount of profits.

First of all, you should convert your e-book into its paperback and audio versions. You can do this on two Amazon's platforms — CreateSpace and ACX. The first one allows you to publish a hard copy of your manuscript for free using a functional print on demand service. ACX, on the other hand, was created to allow writers to produce high-quality audiobooks starting from their creation. You can either pay a narrator upfront (usually the price ranges from 30 to 50 dollars per finished hour) or do royalty split. If you are short on money, splitting royalties with a narrator is a great way to get that extra revenue for free, but if you want to build a huge business, you should definitely pay upfront to get the full benefit.

After you have created and published the audio and paperback version of your book, you can experiment with other publishing channels. Some of our favorite ones are Draft to Digital and PublishDrive. You can even get your book translated into different languages for free through BabelCube, always following a royalty split model.

So, to sum it up, here is the process to publish a book to create a passive income stream.

1. Get the book written by E-Writer Solutions.
2. Get the book cover done on Fiverr.
3. Publish the book on Amazon KDP.
4. Publish the book on CreateSpace.
5. Publish the book on ACX, paying your narrator upfront.

6. Publish your book on Draft to Digital.
7. Publish your book on PublishDrive.
8. Translate your book through Babelcube for free.

This is the script to follow and that is able to create a passive income stream on autopilot. Now that we have covered the general aspects, it is time to see the details of the entire process.

Chapter 3: How to Get a High-quality Cover for Your Book

Many argue that we should not judge a book by its cover, and in principle, we can all agree to this, whether the phrase is used literally speaking of books and even more so if the phrase is used in a metaphorical sense talking about life.

Speaking of books, however, we must take into account that, in the current publishing market where new proposals appear daily, the initial glance can make the difference between attracting a reader and making him curious or leaving him indifferent.

So, if your goal is to sell more copies, then, first of all, you have to accept the fact that your book will be (always) judged by the cover and then strong of this awareness, you have to try to make the best cover possible.

The cover of your book must attract the reader's attention, even if he does not know you and has never heard of you, in fact, especially if he does not know you and has never heard of you and your book.

In all likelihood, your friends and relatives would buy your book even if it has a horrible cover or if it did not have it at all, but your goal must be to widen the circle of your readers. Those who do not know you, who do not know who you are, or who have never heard of you will, therefore, judge your book first of all by the cover whether you like it or not.

The cover of your book is like a shop window, in which the best or rarest products are displayed, indicating the offers, illuminated, and taken care of to attract customers.
The cover, in fact, is the first thing that the reader sees of your book, and this first glance must spark attraction,

curiosity, and interest.

This is why it is so important that you dedicate time to create a beautiful cover for your book, a cover that aligns with the characteristics of the literary genre to which the book belongs while maintaining a recognizable style, a cover that meets the expectations of the market without, however, renouncing your originality.

Three Ways to Make a Beautiful Cover

1. Do it yourself

Making your own cover is definitely the cheapest choice, but it is the riskiest. I recommend it only if you are an expert graphic designer, and when I say expert, I do not mean to say that you occasionally retouch photos of your friends. Making a cover means having much higher graphics skills.

If you download images from the Internet, make sure they are of good quality, especially if you want to make the cover for the paper format of your book because to print a sharp image, you need to start from high-resolution files.

Also, make sure you have the rights of the images you use. If you download the photos for free from the network, make sure they are free to use, perhaps by explicitly asking the owner of the site where you found them.

If, on the other hand, you download photos from image sites (such as Shutterstock), check for what purposes you are authorized to use them. Some images can be used for books or publications only within a certain limit of circulation. Others can be used only with the attribution of credit to the author. In this case, it will suffice to mention the author's name (usually on the back of the title page or on the back cover).

Do not underestimate these checks because it would be a shame to distribute your book and then discover that you have to withdraw it and change the cover because you were not allowed to use an image, or worse, have to pay penalties for copyright infringement.

If you really want to do it yourself, make at least three different versions of your cover and then let others choose the best one.

The problem, in fact, is that you know the contents of the book and you are inevitably conditioned, while the cover must be effective especially in the eyes of those who have not read the book yet and do not even know what it is talking about.

The cover image should not, therefore, be an image that can only be understood after reading the book but rather must communicate a clear message before the book is read and just so that this happens!

This is why the author is usually the least suitable person to determine which cover works best and attracts more readers.

So, if you, as an author, want to try your hand at the cover of your book, create at least three completely different versions of each other (not just three variants) and then subject them to the judgment of other people, friends, relatives, or better, of strangers, who will be freer to give you their sincere judgment.

2. Ask a professional

Some graphic designers have a site where you can see their work, while others have a Facebook page. In any case, my advice is this: Browse through their profiles, look at the exhibited works, and then contact the ones you like the most, those that you feel are more similar to your way of understanding the cover of your book.

You will realize that the prices between American and foreign graphic designers are very different because, generally, American graphic designers are cheaper. This happens because, especially if we look at the US market, there is much more demand, and good graphic designers can ask for higher figures.

If none of the names listed here convince you, you can search the net on numerous freelance sites.

I suggest you take a look at Fiverr.com, an international freelance platform where you can find graphics and much more. You can see for example web designers, webmasters, proofreaders, translators, etc. The prices on Fiverr are very competitive, and for this, it is indeed worth going for a ride through the various profiles to see if you find the one that is right for you.

In this regard, I suggest you not to limit your search only to American freelancers or those who speak English.

Moreover, if it is a matter of doing graphic work, it does not matter if the freelancer working for you understands what is written in your back-cover text. It will be enough for him to copy it as you give it to him and insert it into the image he will create for you.

Do not even limit yourself to the content of your request. Why ask only the cover for the e-book format when, with a few more dollars, you can get the full front/back cover? It does not matter if you have not yet decided whether to publish your book in paper format; meanwhile, you have the cover ready for printing. Moreover, you could ask for the creation of a coordinated graphics project. So, in addition to the cover for your book, you could, for example, get the graphics for your Facebook page or the graphics for your blog or flyers, posters, and bookmarks, all with the same cover image of your book.

3. Start a contest

Launching a graphic contest or a competition between graphic designers is undoubtedly the most expensive choice to create the cover of your book, but it is the one that guarantees you a wider selection of results.

Here are some of the most popular sites that offer graphics contests.

- 99designs
- BestCreativity
- DesignCrowd
- YouCrea
- Leevia
- Zooppa

If you have to contact one by one dozens of graphic designers that you like and ask everyone for a proposal for the cover of your book, it would take you forever, and you would spend a fortune. In a contest, however, you have the advantage that, in a single site and with only one action (the launch of the contest), you can receive proposals from different professionals.

The number of proposals you can receive depends on many factors. First of all, the cash value of the prize to be won, but certainly, in a graphic design contest, you will receive many more proposals than you could obtain with a single graphic designer.

A single professional, in fact, generally offers you one or two ideas or, at most, three, among which you can then choose the one you prefer and only on that one he then defines the details (characters, colors, distribution of the text, etc.).

In a contest, however, you could receive dozens, if not hundreds, of different proposals, which will be very different from each other because they come from various people who have different experiences, tastes, styles, and sensibilities.

Chapter 4: How to Write a Powerful Description

It is vital to ensure that your books are found among a multiplicity of competitors (here comes the SEO on Amazon and advertising campaigns). In fact, after a potential customer clicks on your book, it is important to persuade him to buy your book.

And it is right now that your skills as copywriters come into play!

Writing a bomb-proof Amazon book description is not easy.

So, how to write a book description on Amazon? Here are some useful tips.

1. Understand the needs of your client

It is essential to understand the needs of your client before starting to write the description of your book.

Here are two critical points to consider in writing a perfect description of your book.

- Specific characteristics: We are talking about gender, income, interests, and lifestyle. Browse on Google to connect with sites, blogs, forums, and Facebook groups in the niche you are publishing in.

- Customer reviews: What they want, their concerns, and what they like and do not like matter. Read the reviews of the books of your competitors.

The information you collect will be reflected in each section of the Amazon book description.

In this way, you are certain to build trust and a good relationship with your future clients.

2. Do not be fooled by your competitors

Even if you see that your competitors' books seem to sell a lot of copies, their description might be lacking.

You may not know it, but among books with the Best Seller tag or those with more reviews, you can lose a lot of money a day due to bad conversions.

Not a big deal, then. But how does it happen?

You have to consider the fact that behind the scenes could circulate very cheap discounts (for those who buy) or that the seller is giving away the books in exchange for reviews (all of these are activities against Amazon policies).

Working well and optimizing your book description on Amazon will give you the opportunity to differentiate yourself and gain a long-term competitive advantage.

3. Dedicate the right time to search for keywords

Not all keywords are created equal.

The work you just did to get to know your client was essential to understand the terms that are used to search for books on Amazon.

Keyword research is, therefore, necessary for leading your potential customers to your book listing. Services and software applications like Sonar, MerchantWords, or Keywordtool are your best allies to find the right keywords for your book.

As for the management of the keywords on Amazon, you can include them in the title, in the bullet points, in the description, and in the field of keywords that you find in the backend of the book.

Practical Tips for Writing a Book Description on Amazon

1. Book title

The purpose of the title is to attract the attention of visitors who run the Amazon results page after a search.

So, remember that you have to write for people and not just to cheat the Amazon algorithm and position yourself in SERP.

Do not abuse keywords: Creating a confusing title with many keywords will not help you rank your book, and on the other hand, doing so can reduce your chance to get noticed by readers. Concentrate on creating a catchy title with one or two of your best keywords, not more.

Consider the length of the title: Titles will be seen by potential customers through different tools, and their length might not allow them to be shown in full on smaller screens. Consider that when you create your title.

2. Bulleted lists

The bulleted lists must summarize the most relevant features and the benefits that the customer obtains reading the book.

It is even better if you can concentrate on a single advantage, but the important thing is not to be vague.

Put yourself in the customer's shoes: The bulleted lists are used to solve the doubts and perplexities that every person has before buying a book.

If other versions or books similar to yours have any chronic problems that everyone knows, explain why the solution of your book is the best one compared to them.

3. Description of the book

The description of the book is essential to extend the narration of your book even further in-depth, overcoming the last hesitations of the customer and convincing him to buy the book exactly at that time.

Think about the most persuasive advertisement you've ever seen: In the first few minutes, you are shown to the customer who is facing a specific problem that no books seem to be able to solve. But here, suddenly, the book object of advertisement takes place on the scene, which, in no time at all, solves the problem of the customer.

The objective of the description is, therefore, to show how your book is different or better than the competitors.

Use an informal tone and leverage every important or peculiar aspect of your book.

Some tips for writing a compelling book description are:

- Use mainly active forms.
- Eliminate and avoid using meaningless and abused adjectives like "best," "high-quality," or "evergreen."
- Focus on the benefits that the book provides.

4. HTML formatting

A lot of publishers do not know this, but you can use HTML formatting in the description of your book. This is not an HTML programming guide, but here are the basics that you should know before starting to write your very own description.

Bold = <b>

Italic = <i>

Underline = <u>

To close the tag, you can use </ and the letter of the command you are using >. It is imperative to always close a tag before starting to use another. If you do not select any tag, you will write in the standard paragraph style.

Chapter 5: Keep the Publishing Business Going

Professional Training

As we have seen, passive income exists, but it won't happen immediately.

Unfortunately, however, people who start self-publishing think that, after buying an e-book (even the best one in the world), within two days, they will be the new rich internet gurus. It does not work like that. Above all, if you hope to find an e-book that, with four clicks, will set for you an automatic entry, you are out of the way. Not even this e-book will make you rich if you do not act upon what it teaches.

To be successful in all areas of life, we need a mixture of factors. You can have the best book cover in the world, but if you sell poor information inside, you will hardly be able to take advantage of the second rule of self-publishing — customer loyalty. The first rule is your professional training.

A person who buys your book and finds valid information or valid idea will tend not only to return but also to propose it to other people. On the other hand, a disgruntled person will not only refuse to come back but will talk badly about your site, and the rumors run fast on the net.

But even assuming that you have the most excellent book, with the most beautiful cover and the lowest prices, it may not be enough — you have to know how to sell them. Maybe everything is perfect, but then, you do not know enough to intrigue a user to buy it. The potential customer might go out and buy a book somewhere else, even spending more.

With this, we are not saying that it is impossible to become a self-publisher, but we must consider it as a profession in every sense. If someone thinks of creating a good book and getting rich without having the right skills, he has the wrong mindset. However, if he dedicates the right time for his training, then he can really create a big source of cash flow.

Create Partnerships

It is true that creating friendships, alliances, and partnerships are fundamental. Having people working in your own field of interest near you can be very useful. You can exchange ideas, opinions, and advice. On the other hand, if someone thinks that this kind of alliances can be found between relatives and friends, he will find himself crashing into a wall. Friends and relatives, if not already in the sector, will be the biggest obstacle. They will be the ones who, at every error, will only put their finger in the wound not because they do not love you but because the brain rejects everything that it does not understand. This is why we always suggest to work on your financial goals on your own and to share what you are doing only after getting the first sign of success. Remember that, at the earlier stages, your mindset is very weak and even the slightest critique can make it collapse.

Chapter 6: How to market your book using social media

Do you really need a Social Media Marketing Plan to market your book? The answer is simple, short, and direct— if you do not have a plan, you have little chance of success.

Planning means having a strategy. Without a strategy in the modern market, you will not sell. So, in other words, planning equals selling.

However, is creating a proper Social Marketing Plan for your book easy or difficult? It depends. If it is your first time, you can find some difficulties, but you will see that, in concrete, it is not very far from what you have already done in the past for your business. You have to reflect, compare, hypothesize, choose, understand, enhance, and finally to verify.

Using a metaphor, we could see Marketing as an orchestra and the Social Marketing Plan as the sheet to be followed. Every marketing action is the symphony played by a single musician. The sheet imposes rules, times, and style. The orchestra represents the set of many instruments that play, but they play alternately following a wise strategy. Every musical instrument is important but necessary only if it follows the score. It is the conductor who decides what, when, and why.

Now, are you ready to make a Social Media Marketing Plan for your book? Did you understand the need? To make a good plan to market your book, you have to follow these 6 steps. They will simplify your life.

Step 1: Identify the Correct Goals

The first step for any marketing strategy for a book is to establish the goals you are hoping to achieve. The more you have clear objectives to achieve, the easier it will be to meet them or react quickly to changes in the market and business strategies. Without a concrete objective, there is no means to measure the progress of a marketing campaign. These Social goals must, of course, be aligned with the broader marketing strategy.

One of the most used methods to identify the correct objective to pursue is the SMART approach. SMART is an acronym used to remember the 5 characteristics of the correct goal— specific (specific), measurable (measurable), attainable, pertinent (relevant), limited in time (time-bound, with a fixed expiration).

An easy way to start your social media marketing plan is to give yourself at least 2 to 3 small goals. For example, you decide that you will share photos about the topic of the book on Instagram. You will do this by posting 3 pictures a week with the goal of getting at least 30 shares a week and 10 comments. In addition, post your short articles on Facebook (at least twice a week). It would be better if they are related to the content on your book or niche because you can directly link them and receive more visits. All activities must have a pre-established time and must be measurable and measured.

Step 2: Market Analysis and Competition Analysis

The second step is to do a real market analysis of what can be done on every single social network and what your competitors are doing, obviously taking inspiration from international success stories, perhaps from your own sector.

Step 3: Voice and Style

Each company has its own style and its own image that is usually reflected in every action — how the sales show up, the stand presented at the fair, the brochures, the business cards, the website, and so on. The company cannot communicate; it merely does so with its headquarters and warehouse through furniture, colors, and its logo. The actions on Social must invariably convey the style and the image that the company has strategically chosen to deliver.

The Marketing Manager must be able to make social users perceive what the company wants them to perceive.

Step 4: The Tools and the Channels

When you are well aware of the company style to communicate, all you need to do is identify the tools and channels you want to use.

Among the tools, we must obviously include the web tools that were born in recent years dedicated to the editorial management of content on social media. Well-known tools such as Hootsuite, TweetDeck, ManageFlitter, and many others are essential for the management and analysis of social marketing.

Step 5: Content Plan

The fifth step gives you the opportunity to reassemble all the previous steps in a single tool, creating a real Content Plan, with precise timing divided by days, weeks, and months.

The editorial calendar must reflect the identified objectives, the chosen market strategy, the company style, and the pre-established tools/channels.

For example, if your purpose on Instagram is to generate contacts and the one on Facebook simply to communicate the corporate image, you must make sure that your calendar represents well these two objectives (in terms of timing, type of message, tool used, editorial consistency over time, and the number of weekly posts).

Step 6: Constant Check

Having implemented a Social Marketing Plan with its editorial strategy, it becomes crucial to be able to measure its progress and success, perhaps even ROI (return on investment). Also, for this step, as for the fourth, it is essential to use dedicated tools, particularly Google Analytics (analysis Blog, Website, Newsletter, Landing pages, etc.). For some time, Twitter has also been offering its Analytics for free. These and other tools allow you to analyze, in detail, a large amount of data grouped by type, bringing a clear picture of what works and what does not, which social leads to more visits to the website, and which others are able to turn them into active contacts (customers).

After you have created the perfect marketing plan for your book, the next step is to apply it and start creating and posting content. Social media marketing is one of the best ways to generate more sales and build an audience of readers that will fall in love with your book. This process will give you the ability to leverage your followers for the next release so that the second book will immediately find a group of potential customers. You can now see how easy it is to build a successful publishing business when you put together the right publishing strategies with the best marketing ideas. If you provide your followers with great books, you will be on your way to build a self-publishing empire.

Small- and medium-sized self-publishing businesses can use Facebook marketing strategies with high margins of success. In fact, with more than 2 billion active users every month, it is impossible to remove the blue social from your web marketing plan for your book.

How to Use Facebook at Its Best

Brand awareness

Facebook is a vital tool that enables small- and medium-sized publishing businesses to make their books known, while at the same time cultivating a very direct relationship with interested users.

If, on the one hand, your community, made up of people who already know your books, can follow you on the blue social, on the other side, it is possible to reach people who do not know you through spontaneous sharing or through sponsored ones. The latter, through the creation of the right audience, allow reaching to new people potentially interested in our books.

Customer care

Facebook is also one of the websites that best lend themselves to customer care, which is assistance to its customers. Indeed, given the announcement of future updates of the algorithm of the views of the News Feed, focusing on customer care could also prove to be successful in terms of awarding the content posted.
Promotional content can still be valid, but using your own social page as a place to solve problems and perplexities of its users can be a key that you can use often because it is able to trigger conversations between friends, debates, and an engagement appreciated by Facebook algorithms.

Direct sales

Facebook can also be used to sell your books. Like an e-commerce site, the platform lends itself to the possibility of direct purchase from the page, with huge benefits for users. For small- and medium-sized self-publishing businesses, this opportunity is an important resource for saving resources that would otherwise have to be spent on the creation and management of an entire site.
Obviously, it must be said that those who hold an important publishing business cannot simply rely on the social network of Zuckerberg to market their books online. However, it is a fact that not a month passes in which the Menlo Park team does not make the availability of some new functions favor those who want to sell via the web.

How to Create a Facebook Marketing Strategy That Works?

Before starting to take action on Facebook, it is good for small- and medium-sized self-publishing businesses to devote time to creating a well-designed communication plan.

First of all, the goals of the strategies to be put in place must be defined.

Secondly, the public must be identified, that is, the buyer, the typical customer, tracing a sort of identikit of its main characteristics such as age, place of residence, interests, level of education, and more.

As for the content, it will be good to dedicate only 20% of them to the promotion of your books so as not to tire the user with continuous offers and hype.

Finally, the tools for checking the results must not be forgotten, with the choice of the most appropriate metrics to follow in order to understand the effectiveness of the steps taken along the road to achieving the designated objectives. For example, if the setting up of a valid customer care campaign has been done, one of the ways to evaluate the effectiveness of the actions carried out is the analysis of the number and quality of comments received, rather than that of "likes."

Facebook for Small Publishing Businesses

Why should you use Facebook to market your small publishing business?

Facebook is about to touch the ceiling of a billion users according to the latest official data released in July. The number of people who connect to this social network are 955 million every month and 552 million every day; this is more than half a billion of daily users who connect to Facebook with a mobile device - mobile phone, smartphone, tablet.

Facebook is becoming, for many, a major source of

information more and more often, instead of connecting to the homepage of newspapers to see what is happening. We scroll the dashboard reading and commenting on the news linked by our friends. The 2011 CENSIS report on the American company shows that Facebook is used as a source of information by 26.8% of Americans, a percentage that grows to 61.5% in the age group of 14 to 29 years.

The quantity and nature of our relationships have been radically changed by the possibility of keeping in touch with people we do not see daily in person, but for the most diverse circumstances, we feel close. They were our friends in the past, shared a travel experience or studied with, or met online and subsequently met live.

Facebook allows us to listen and exchange opinions, information, points of view, emotions, creating and impetuous dynamic of conversations. This is an open bar where people pass from one group to another, participating in dozens of discussions. The companies suddenly find themselves "degraded" to one voice among others, which must gain attention thanks to the importance of what it says without the possibility of massively occupying the spaces of visibility. Furthermore, we must learn to speak "with" people, which means, first of all, to listen and respond.

Should your publishing business have a presence on Facebook? In the vast majority of cases, the answer is yes. Do not fall into the trap of thinking that Facebook is exclusively the realm of lazy people; often times, it is a great way to "feel the pulse" of your stakeholders and can intercept your needs and opportunities that otherwise you would not have known.

An active presence on Facebook can help you:
- Increase your visibility, spreading your books all over the internet;
- Establish a more intense relationship with your customers, better knowing their needs and obtaining

important feedback on what you do;
- Motivate and gratify your "super fans";
- Promote and share initiatives, special offers, and new books.

Facebook Marketing Ads for Small Publishing Businesses

Each Facebook campaign consists of 3 levels, and it starts from the campaign level, which includes one or more ad groups. As you have just read, for each campaign you create, you will have to choose a goal. This is the real distinctive factor at the campaign level.

At the Ad Group level (Ad Set), you will have to choose the target, the available budget, the publication times, the offer, and the placements (placements). Going down the hierarchy, at the level of the announcements, you can set the type of announcement (image, video, carousel, etc.), all the texts, the call-to-action (action button), and the destination links.
As mentioned, the structure is hierarchical, so if you pause (or delete), for example, a group of ads, the same thing will happen to all ads below that group.

The Definition of the Goals

Now that we understand the structure of a Facebook campaign and the parameters needed to be set for each level, we are ready to launch our first campaign.

The first question is, therefore, "What is the goal to be achieved?"
Do you want to sell a particular book because maybe you have an e-commerce store besides Amazon, want to create awareness or reputation, or do you want to have leads?

Often, in a complete web marketing strategy, we will have to create different campaigns for the different phases of the purchasing process. We can then create different ads depending on whether the target user does not know our brand or knows it but does not know our book or, for example, knows our books and may be interested in a commercial offer.

Facebook itself, in the creation phase, will propose you different objectives divided into 4 macro-categories; let's see them in detail one by one.

Brand awareness

When to use it: in large-scale campaigns, when there is not a particular action that you want to take to the user. This goal will be more attractive to large companies that can afford to launch campaigns for pure branding. For smaller publishing businesses, however, almost every other objective will give better and more significant results.

Reach

When to use it: to reach the maximum number of users to which the ad will show. With the introduction of the rules, Facebook now allows you to put a cap on the frequency with which the advertisement is shown to the same user; in this sense, the goal for reach becomes very useful when you have to work with a relatively small audience, and you want everyone to view the ad.

Traffic

When to use it: when we want to take users to a website or, for example, on a landing page. It is a very interesting goal when promoting content, such as a free book.

Leads

When to use it: to simplify the signup process from mobile devices. When someone clicks on the ad, a form opens with all personal contact information already pre-filled based on the information they share on Facebook, such as name, surname, phone, and email address. This aspect makes the process really fast with just 2 clicks, one to open the ad and one to send the information.

The only problem with this type of objective is that, often, the email address used to sign up for Facebook several years ago is obsolete and has not been updated for too long. In this case, we would get a useless contact. As a result, it has been observed that better conversion campaigns perform that point to specific external landing pages with data to be filled out.

Another aspect to keep in mind is that lead ads do not allow you to include all the information you want in the offer, like on a landing page. Therefore, for campaigns that require a great deal of cognitive attention from the user, a campaign for conversions will be more successful.
With that said, in any case, it is always better to do a test between the two approaches and see which performs better because each case and sector can behave differently.

The success of a Facebook campaign depends almost entirely on how we select the right target. Good results are not obtained by trying to guess the interests but only by experimenting and testing and knowing the right tools.

1. The pixel of Facebook

Mark Dellano, a Facebook expert, is categorical: the pixel of Facebook should always be installed anyway, even if, at the moment, we are not interested in using it for the promotion of our publishing business and if we believe we do not need anything. But, why? Because when it is installed (by entering a code on our personal page), it starts recording data. The pixel will then be able to make us reach users who come into contact with our book selection, and these users can be used in future for our listings. It must be installed "regardless" because we may regret not having collected the data when these will help us.

2. Spy on competitors' sponsorships

Coming into an advertisement published by our competitors can be a golden opportunity. We can "spy" the target they have chosen for their sponsorship. Just click on "Why do I view this ad?" and the magic is accomplished: We will see exactly what target our competitor has set.

If the interests that our competitor has selected works we do not know, we can still get an idea based on the vanity metrics, and in any case, we now have some tools to test.

3. Create a personalized audience

Facebook gives us many options to intercept our potential customers, and we should always start with our customers or our traffic. For example, we can take advantage of the pixel and select who visits specific pages of our book e-commerce site or generate events (such as sales or add to cart), who spends more time on the website or who visits it more often, and who opens the newsletter.

4. Take advantage of other channels, like AdWords

The ads on Facebook certainly do not answer to any conscious question. We launch the bait to a potentially interested public and hope that someone will realize that they need our book. With ads on AdWords, instead, we intercept the conscious need: The user needs the tires and searches on Google, finds our ad, and lands on our site.

Well, we can take advantage of the results obtained from AdWords. Just leave the pixel of Facebook "listening" and with the data obtained create our custom audience based on traffic on the book page. At that point, the user, who has seen our model X of tires but who has not completed the purchase, will see "chased" from our book even within Facebook.

5. Use A/B testing

The analysis of the results obtained must always be exploited to our advantage. Facebook gives us the opportunity with A/B testing.

Facebook Campaigns: Rules to Define the Budget

The risk of wasting money on Facebook campaigns is very high. To avoid spending our money badly, a series of precautions that it is best to undertake.

Here are some rules to improve CPAs (cost per action) by working on the budget:

Do not choose too ambitious self-optimization goals. This is especially true for e-commerce, but it is always applicable. It takes a number of daily conversions high enough for campaigns to be able to learn effectively and improve their performance. We use micro-conversions, i.e., intermediate conversions, that are easier to obtain.

Head different configurations (see advanced planning). When the available budget allows it and "we are allowed to make mistakes," it is good to test different configurations in order to find the ideal setting.

Increase the budget progressively. When a campaign proves to be performing well, it is normal to want to increase the budget allocated to it and make it climb; however, the increase must be progressive and for small steps (10% -20%). If there is urgency, better clone the campaign and create a new one with the desired budget. Otherwise, there is a 9/10 chance of increase in CPC and a general decline in the performance.

Do not accept default placements. Always separate positions in groups with the same target until proven otherwise.

Facebook Leads: How to Get Quality Leads

Do not stop at the lead, and look for the quality of the contact. Landing pages generate higher-quality contacts because they intercept the aware questions and require commitment to fill out the forms, and the quality is paid (with CPL, costs per lead, high).

The Facebook lead ads have unparalleled CPLs, but the quality is affected. The Facebook form is pre-filled with the user's data, and often, the latter submits without giving weight to the action, perhaps even just out of curiosity. That's why with the ads should never be used insertions and forms too simple.

Indeed, complex forms, in which we challenge the user with questions (or even propose a quiz), can have a considerable engagement.

Among the various platforms in which to start implementing social media marketing activities, Facebook tends to be one that best meets the marketing goals of your self-publishing business.

Common Mistakes for Beginners

The main reason is represented by an imposing and transversal critical mass (over 122 million users in America) that is unmatched in any other social network, within which a large part of its potential audience is likely to be present.

If we add to this a very low access threshold (you can monetize already sustained media investments such as photos, articles, videos, etc.) and some interesting advertising possibilities, it becomes easy to see how the Californian colossus has become one of the favorite platforms worldwide.

Precisely, with the advantages listed, however, planning an editorial activity on a corporate Facebook page can become a source of clamorous mistakes, misunderstandings with its customers, and gaffes that are difficult to remedy, capable of shaking even the most authoritative brands.

In this chapter, we list some of the major mistakes that any self-publishing business about to start a promotion of their books on Facebook should keep in mind and try to avoid.

1. Not having a strategy

People's own content page is an activity that, to bring concrete results, must be programmed with accuracy, according to criteria of efficiency (e.g., availability of multimedia material) and effectiveness (e.g., contents that stimulate the involvement of users), creating the mix that best lends itself to boost your audience and reach the set goals.

Basing its presence solely on the dissemination of commercial content, for example, with repeated links to books, it is one of the temptations in which it is not only easier to fall but also which only results in the early loss of interest in the book brand by their fans.

2. Not having defined goals

Improvisation is, in particular in the field of social media marketing and is one of the mistakes most often made by companies usually because of the apparent ease of use of many platforms and/or tools.

This rule also applies to Facebook: Approaching the platform without having considered the most appropriate strategy to follow and without having first defined clear, specific and measurable objectives to pursue, means starting an activity that will be completely same, if not counterproductive.

3. Not having a posting schedule

Finding the right timing to publish your updates is an essential element to determine your visibility on Facebook. Understanding the most correct frequency indeed requires some time (and attempts) since it varies according to the relevant public (there is no rule applicable to all).

In this way, however, we will be able to maximize the visibility of our posts, avoiding too large editorial "holes" or, on the contrary, clogging the Home Page of our contacts with too close updates, with the risk of losing the acquired fans and coming "hidden" "from the respective news flows.

Common Mistakes for Intermediates

When you are an intermediate-level self-publisher, there are two main mistakes that you risk to make on Facebook. Correcting them as soon as possible is the first step to get to the next level.

1. Do not remember the balance between performance and results

We find that mentally splitting the campaign objectives between performance and results is the most effective starting point.

Remember? In Facebook, "performance" is what the campaign level aims to increase the yield in terms of Likes, Comments, Shares, and Reproductions of content that come from social media. On the other hand, "results" goes to cover all those campaigns that aim to bring the user on the site and monitor, possibly, conversions.

This is the enormous strength of Facebook, being able to

tap into a social context to direct people to an external page, like your book page on Amazon, or vice-versa.

Thus, some of the questions to be asked become:
- When do I need to track the performance of a Facebook content?
- When do I need to track results, in terms of leads collected on a landing?

In this sense, collecting Likes for a brand page becomes just a piece of the puzzle. A campaign with this goal is just the first step to deliver a targeted editorial strategy to this fan base or maybe use this audience in a second campaign, this time with the goal "Address people to your website" or develop a similar audience again.

In the same way, increasing the visualizations of a video allows you to think first of the performance (the reproductions obtained, of course) and on a horizon to results, building a list of audiences based precisely on the percentages of reproduction.

Before thinking about ad creativity, mentally divide the opportunities given by Facebook in terms of performance and results is the best (and really strategic) way to proceed.

2. Ignore the new features

One of the best adjectives to describe Facebook Ads is "seething," with its eternal modification and improvement. New features are screaming loudly, especially among industry professionals. In other cases, they pass undertone or are released in installments without precise timing.

Taking advantage of the opportunities offered by any new ad setup or bidding mechanics is especially important when it comes to refinements that are still young, of which we do not know any future of, but that could bring interesting results. Arriving first, in this case, is an opportunity not to be missed.

Common Mistakes for Advanced Self-Publishers That Use Facebook

1. Not being reactive

Do not assume that what works today can continue to do so without changes in the coming times. Be ready to push (even at the budget level) what works, seizing the opportunities when they arise.

Come back to your campaigns as often as possible, look at reports critically, and above all, be ready to change your mind. Not always the most creative advertisement is the one that converts the best. Not always the call-to-action that you have retouched for a long time is the most effective. The ego has nothing to do with it: you only look at the results.

2. Not dividing the campaign by placements

Facebook does its best to give as much exposure as possible to its advertisers' ads. However, this visibility does not always coincide with the best context to make our message effective.

Dividing each campaign at least between desktop and mobile is the basis for avoiding the dispersion of the message across multiple fronts. Refine the message between smartphone and tablet on the next step.

With the progressive development of Facebook Ads, it is not uncommon to find campaigns automatically addressed to the news feed on desktop, mobile, tablet, within Instagram, and on the audience network. Separate, as much as possible, each front with different creatives and approaches — even at the budget level.

Some advice?

- The desktop news feed is great for generating engagement since it supports longer texts and more readable descriptions.
- The mobile news feed is more useful to reach a target that does not yet know us, bringing the first click on a landing and allowing us to act in remarketing in the medium term.
- The right-hand column is always less efficient, but often cheaper and still useful in remarketing contexts.
- The audience network is interesting as an opportunity to collect clicks from in-target users, but it is scarcely relevant to point directly to conversions.
- The positioning on Instagram is everything to test niche for niche, but realistically it can work better on more emotional contexts.

3. Not testing different creatives and levers

Not all messages work the same way, especially when there is not a real campaign historian or other marketing strategies that can provide a canvas are not active. The real challenge is to grasp which "form" has the ideal announcement for those who receive it.

Experimenting, in this case, is a must. Head different images, with different tones, with or without people inside. Evaluate more or less long texts and the presence or absence of links. Change the call-to-action present under the content (if the campaign goal allows it). Finally, Different colors with different intensities could bring out or bury your ad regardless of the message.

Do not just offer a single ad and see clicks, conversions, and cost reports arrive. It is not satisfactory. The goal is to understand what is the best cost/result ratio that can be achieved and with which creativity.

Conclusion

Thank you for making it to the end of this book. I hope it was able to provide you with all the tools that you need to achieve your financial goals.

The next step is to get started with what you have learned throughout this book. Remember, always start with a demo account — become a profitable trader before putting your money on the table.

I hope that you find these lessons valuable and that you got the information you were looking for. Creating a "passive income lifestyle" that works for you will give you an incredible feeling, especially at the beginning when you make the first gains. I am thrilled for you to start and I cannot wait to see your results coming in.

www.ingramcontent.com/pod-product-compliance
Lightning Source LLC
Chambersburg PA
CBHW030540220526
45463CB00007B/2913